DRUNKEN SAILOR

JOHN MONTAGUE

Wake Forest University Press

Wake Forest University Press

Printed in the United States of America
Library of Congress Catalogue Number 2004112243
ISBN (cloth) 1-930630-19-0
ISBN paper) 1-930630-18-2

First published in Ireland by The Gallery Press
(Peter Fallon, Editor)

DRUNKEN SAILOR

Contents

part one
White Water *page* 13
The Hag's Cove 14
Roethke's Ghost at Roche's Point 17
Hermit 18
Last Resort, Normandy 19
Coast Road 21
The Absent Limb 22
Sea Bed 25
Horizons 26

part two
Letter Valley
1 Mary Kate's Kitchen 29
2 Scribe in the Woods 29
3 Replay 30
Head or Harp 31
Pilgrims 32
The Deer Trap 33
Clabber: The Poet at Three Years 34
Heart Land 35
West Cork Annunciation 36
Prodigal Son 37
A Holy Show 40
Elements of the Luberon 41
A Fertile Balance 42
Demolition Ireland 45
The Listeners: Elizabeth's Dream 46
Last of the House 47

part three
Legerdemain 51
Scraping the Pot 52
Family Rosary 53

Wreaths
   1 A Good Bye 55
   2 Civil War Veteran 55
Grave Song 56
Last Court 57
First Landscape, First Death 61
Slievemore 64

part four
   The Plain of Blood 69

Acknowledgements and Notes 78

In memory of
Seán Lucy, poet and teacher,
who brought me to Cork,
and Turlough Montague, my brother,
with whom I played, long ago,
in a Brooklyn park . . .

At seventy-five I have understood better the structure of nature, of animals, plants, trees, birds, fishes and insects. Consequently, at the age of eighty, I should have made more progress; at ninety, I should penetrate the mystery of things; at a hundred I should have reached a remarkable stage; and at one hundred and ten everything I do, every point and line, would be as a living thing . . .

— Written at the age of seventy-five years by me, formerly Hokusai, the old man, mad about drawing

Two things fill the mind with increasing awe and reverence, the more one reflects: the starry heavens above, the moral law within.
— Kant, *The Critique of Practical Reason*

PART ONE

White Water

for Line McKie

The light, tarred skin
of the currach rides
and receives the current,
rolls and responds to
the harsh sea swell.

Inside the wooden ribs
a slithering frenzy; a sheen
of black-barred silver-
green and flailing mackerel:
the iridescent hoop
of a gasping sea trout.

As a fish gleams most
fiercely before it dies,
so the scales of the sea-hag
shine with a hectic
putrescent glitter:

luminous, bleached —
white water —
that light in the narrows
before a storm breaks.

The Hag's Cove

Over the steeped, heaped seaweed
the flies, shimmering blue-black
and gold, sing their song of harvesting,
of dissolution, the necessary process
of putrefaction, decay's deadly drone.

Thick dragons' tails of wrack,
frilled flutter of dulse,
a song of things breaking down,
other things feeding upon them,
a compost heap of dissolving forms,
a psalm, a threnody of decomposition.

❖

I made my way there, daily,
a sort of dark pilgrimage,
mind and body freshening
after the habitual soilings,
(tensions of work, family,
ceaseless sour quarrels),
soothed by the ocean's
eternal turning flange,
its vast devouring indifference,
blue and calm, or bruised and folding
with angry, heaving motion.

❖

Along the promontory
stand three stone towers,
not only 'dead at the top'
but hollowed, useless, except
as a sanctuary for wild animals,

for nestling birds, or lovers
fleeing the constant coastal rains.

Such a long time since compass,
spyglass and binoculars
watched and waited for
the great Atlantic liners,
Cunard and White Star,
carrying their cargo of pain away
(torn families, old-fashioned exile tears)
or, laden with success, returning
(the glossy suit of the prodigal son):
looming shapes at the mouth
of Cork's verdant, unfurling harbour.

❖

One smashed down here, below,
a Captain drunk in his bunk
as his charge rammed the rocks;
caught and tossed all day
between the Cow and the Calf,
slowly smashed into smithereens;
now a hushed pub legend.

❖

To allow oneself to be swallowed again,
repossessed by nature's thick sweetness
(Over the steeped, heaped seaweed
the flies sing their song of harvesting),
that hectic glitter of decay,
that gluttonous moil of creation,
to be smashed on the rocks,
broken down and built again,

clutching at the intimate softness
of tough reed, brave flower,
swaying at the cliff's edge,
like the mind on its fraying tether;
what shall we do with *this drunken sailor*
early in the morning?

Roethke's Ghost at Roche's Point

The sea checks its waves
from the rocks to watch.
The wind stills its breath
in the trees to catch
the echo of his clumsy steps

as he & his shadow turn,
a figure glowing on its own,
where sky and ocean join
in a light bleached and
wild as scoured bone.

The ghosts of fish
lift from chill depths
to swell the silent throng:
slithering dogfish, furled
seahorse, curled conger;

verdigris mackerel,
with gulping gills,
leap from their nets
flailing fins over
the face of the water.

Birds halt in the sky,
turn frantic somersaults,
a seagull feints to fall
from a deep wall of rock,
and now, that flaring cry —

as the night finds tongue
(all the living to come,
all the dead long gone)
under the driving moon
by the lighthouse dome.

Hermit

The night structures swarm-
ing around this attic room;
a silver trellis of stars,
tide wash, then silence.

Stir and creak of the fire,
an ikon bright on the wall
and, of course, books, papers,
hosts of silent dialogue.

To work intently while
the constellations shift
across the frost-sharp sky,
moisture condenses on the glass.

Autumn yielding to winter,
Pegasus to the Hunter,
one year into another,
endless death, ceaseless birth,

while ships toil up the channel,
patient as the night prowl
of the owl, or probing heron;
the snail progress of a poem.

Intellect and universe
held briefly in tune,
under the blanched helm
of the cliff lighthouse,

upright and defiant
against the night,
a restless arm of light
shearing the dark.

Last Resort, Normandy

for Anthony Sheridan

'There was an old woman
who lived in a *blockhaus*';
she was so slatternly
she didn't know what to do:

haunting the summer colony,
Mon Repos, Sans Souci.
A spectre, muttering, grubby,
a chain across her door
to foil the intruder,
a mangy Alsatian
to snarl at holiday visitors,

that new invasion fleet
arrayed on the strand,
glossing their indolent
limbs with lotion.

Summer mermaids
comb tendrils of hair
over bared breasts
while their children
splash in the shallows,
amass sandcastles,

and she spreads
lines of washing
loosely on bushes,
threadbare underwear,
a workingman's shirt,

as her drunken lover
clambers out, blinking,
to pee furiously
into the festive sea.

Coast Road

The speedometer
trembling on
passing sixty
the suck of
hidden waves
rocks humped
like seals in
thick mist as
the pendulum
of the wiper
works to clear
a triangle of
gloomy road
tears divid-
ing your face
as we ride
into, through
the storm.

The Absent Limb

1

The one-legged adulterer
is driving home along
the seacoast road.

Satisfied as a hen,
his postmistress mistress
has snuggled into bed
beside her snoring husband.

2

Everyone knows their story
with the wry acceptance,
amused complicity, of country places;
this sleeping sea-walled village
a coiling nest of Sophoclean
enormities, incest and lust
ransacking the fragile bodies
of the aged, the barely pubescent.

And the sea washes
away everything.

3

But this night is different.
A storm is surging
near the weather station.
Gale force nine and still rising.
A wet whirling darkness
like a vast seashell,

gobbets of spume flying,
the trees straining.

And now the long alley
of the murdered priest
behind locked estate gates;
a predatory family crest.
The wind swirls, murderously.
The tall trees sway over his car,
split and crash on the road.

He cuts the engine
and waits for the last
branch, a terrible judgement,
to topple across the bonnet;
he remembers the lobster
scrabbling in his pot,
fish flailing in his net.

4

But a cleansed dawn breaks.
He drags back branches,
rolls dislodged stones,
manoeuvres a path home
above wrinkling whitecaps.

His absent leg twitches.
He is still alive. And
nature is not a moralist.
When he wakes in the afternoon
the storm has blown.

The sea is calm and light
as laundered linen
or a shriven conscience.

Sea Bed

after an image by Gerard Dillon

When the beloved with
his cargo of dreams
floats in my arms

the fronds of hair
on the nape of his neck,
the hull of his ribcage,

the coral reef
of bone sheathed
beneath wrist, elbow,

seem a marine
statement, more precious,
vulnerable, than any of

his daily affairs,
his ordinary cares,
& his body's length,

rising & falling
with every sigh
and shift of mine,

glints like a star-
fish splayed
on a tidal strand.

Horizons

Dimness of a coast,
a necklace of islands
strewn offshore;
through the mist I glimpse
Hy Brasil, the Eternal West.

❖

Our houses, our loves;
sheets of water glint
on a white sandy shore,
dissolving with the tide,
renewed again
with the waxing of the moon.

PART TWO

Letter Valley

1 mary kate's kitchen

The gate scringes upon its hollowed stone.

I feel I have stumbled back into my own:
old men brooding before a metal hearth,
women bustling between pantry and oilcloth,
a moon-faced wall clock and display of delph,
the girlish gravitas of the Virgin on her shelf.

A long way round to curve near home again,
kindling embers of a long-smoored self.

2 scribe in the woods

after the Irish, 9th century

The birds sing on summer evenings.
A cheeky robin balances on the buoyant bough
of its favourite lichened tree, outside my window,
whistling away, while here comes
a ragged convoy of crows
with their clatter, their funereal flapping home
to the higher branches.

After so many years, I cannot translate
a word they are saying, signals they're exchanging.
Long conferences on telephone wires:
twittered alarms, melodious monotony,
notes arrayed along a staff,
while human messages course ceaselessly
beneath their taut claws.

3 replay

The fuchsia hedge trembles.
Peer closely. All those small
scarlet petals are shivering:
a mass of bells silently pealing,
where the honeybees are clambering;
like uniformed schoolboys swarming
up the slope to Armagh Cathedral.
Or a more profane, modern image,
striped players ceaselessly scoring
inside those green and scarlet meshes
while the whole hedge trembles.

Head or Harp

The butt is a flat round stone.
The marker, a stroke in the dust.
Toecap to the line, sly ones thrust
their upper bodies forward, heron-tilted,
as the *pingin*, or penny, sails aloft
to urgent shouts and curses. Then silence
as eyes strain to see where two
copper coins fall equidistant.

Time for the stand-off —
Padna Hyland steadies the tosser,
two coins balanced on a sliver of wood.
Those small circles are hurled high,
tumbling briefly against the twilight sky.
Then necks crane, peering down again.
Head, or hen? Or Irish harp?
(Across the border, a British crown.)

Voices soften in the darkness,
even oaths are muffled by half-light,
as a thin rain starts to fall,
and the little stream whispers by.
Oh, the melancholy of Midland days!
In the thistled meadow beyond
the becalmed wreck of the Protestant church
a donkey raises its rusty bray.

Pilgrims

A warm summer evening, near Multyfarnham.
Two young pilgrims, on their way home
from the all-night vigil of the Mission
short-cut down the railway line.
Near dawn, they drop their shriven heads down
on the rails. To die like Elizabethans,
two torsos yielding two bright crowns.

The Deer Trap

There was a cave I visited, beside Barney Horisk's bog bank, a small wet cavern with a lattice of branches plaited over. It was near a stream, the insistent Garvaghey River, rattling over its pebbles. I would climb slowly down, and ease myself into this secret space, to sit there for hours in the semi-darkness, with shorts, and bare earth-caked feet. Crouched, legs drawn up, arms folded like fins across my narrow ribs, no sound but my own breathing; nothing to see but glints of sky through the plaited branches, and the silver scrawls of snails down the turf walls.

What was I waiting for? The surprise of a head peering in, a head wearing antlers, the crash of a companion suddenly joining me as it collapses, shuddering, to its knees? We had come on it when we were digging turf, and felt it was different, something connected with faraway times. Men had driven down from the Ministry, carrying instruments and maps, and they had declared it was a deer trap, a deer pit; perhaps from the days when the *Fianna* had hunted their quarry through the great forests?

I hear the cold metal horns, I hear the hoarse cry of the hunting pack, the halloo of men on horses. For I am the hind crouched in darkness, breath rasping, hoping they will never find me, hoping to be found. A small rain begins to trickle down my back . . .

Clabber: The Poet at Three Years

after the Irish of Cathal Ó Searcaigh

'That's clabber! Clutching clabber
sucks caddies down,' said my father harshly
while I was stomping happily
in the ditch on the side of the road.
'Climb out of that clabber pit
before you catch your death of it!'

But I went on splattering and splashing,
and scattering whoops of joy:
'Clabber! Clabber! I belong to it,'
although the word meant nothing to me
until I heard a squelch in my wellies
and felt through every fibre of my duds
the cold tremors of awakening knowledge.

O elected clabber, you chilled me to the bone.

Heart Land

after the Irish

Would you like to

hide in	the thicket of gold?
halt on	the hill of the foxes?
quarrel in	the fortress of shouting?
tumble into	the place of curses?
stride upon	the moor of the hawk?
listen on	the ridge of the seagull?

West Cork Annunciation

The Angel of the Lord declared unto Mary,
and she conceived of the Holy Ghost . . .

An austere kitchen, darker than the fields.
The Angelus sounds through the room.
Silently responding to its measured boom
Mary Kate interrupts our rambling talk
to bless herself, while Jackie doffs the big cap.

People of the past, grown tortoise-slow,
their world will have gone before they do.
Once hens flurried around the scullery door,
once the dog curled before the fire.
Now we sit, mesmerized, solemn,
drawn into the glow of the television.

An opulence of images invades the farmhouse,
girlish ikons from mediaeval France;
Sienese gravity: Raphael's rosy ecstasy.
What harm in this young Jewish bride,
pivot of their peasant world, her peasant child?
Would all our passions were as mild!

A turtle withdrawing into its shell,
Jackie puts back the cap; Mary Kate sighs,
thinking of something she can do for others,
tea to wet, or a whiskey glass to proffer;
she creaks across the room like a sailing ship.
And the Word was made flesh, and dwelt amongst us.

Prodigal Son

MacKillion, my first master of language,
calling, cursing the cattle at twilight
across the enfolding fields,
was a ritual, regular as a blessing,
challenging the silver peal of the Angelus

sounding through my aunts' Catholic kitchen
all the way from Athlone's *Radio Éireann*.
Big John loosed a stream of abuse:
'Big-arsed Polly, / I'll split your belly,'
as he beat them from the corners of the field,

battering their flanks with his big stick,
swaying *elders* swollen with milk.
'Big-diddied devil, / you're a right haveril.'
Their response, as hooves clattered on
the concrete yard, a splatter of dung.

Ganch, gulderer, gulpin, it rang,
a language hard, Northern, profane,
but with its own driving rhythm.
I wondered from what source it sprang,
and was my orphaned lot the same?

Carnaptious, cuttie and *caddie,*
I relished this new vocabulary,
scurrying home in my 'knickerbockers'
from 'the next block', to tell my *weemen*
I'd *bin kepping* the cows from the corn.

❖

Long ago he had been taken in
by our neighbours, staunch Presbyterian.
To give a Catholic bye-child a home,
a tacit custom of that place and time,
rarely held to question, though

once old Mrs Clarke rebuked me when,
agent of my pious aunts, I accused them
of keeping him away from Mass:
'I would never come between
any man and his religion.'

❖

Loneliest of all, Big John
on the haggard wall at dusk, crooning
to himself *Drimindrew*, 'the tune
the old cow died of,' he said:
that harsh lament echoed in my head

against the picture of him all alone
beneath a sky grown brighter than
the twilight-grey whitewashed wall.
But why did he sing that solitary song
in the gloaming, amidst the corn?

Years later I learnt it was a rune,
an *aisling*. An old Jacobite song,
An Droimeann Dubh, The Black
Cow, wandering forlorn through
the dew-wet fields of Ireland. But

innocence can undo anything.
As old age broke him slowly down
my aunts bribed and baited him
with a horn rosary, from this child's hand,
to rope his soul to its Papish home.

Too late I realized the damage done
as Big John marched past our window
to kneel, cramped as a draught horse,
in the chill Confession Box;
a chastened Prodigal Son.

A Holy Show

for Kathleen Raine

Maybe John Scotus was the first to find out how
to lift that non-existent freight of Western thought
a simple echo
of what the creators of the stone circles felt
lofting those tall shapes in the moonlight
the curve of planet earth
on which they briefly dwelt

with all those bright whirling worlds without.
No Platonic cave but a sparkling inside & out,
the air so champagne clear
they could have reached to grasp a star
through the crystalline atmosphere, like a candle
or the rush-light burning in their
neighbour's hut next door.

So the soul will sail when its time has come
to quit its earthly sheath and wander around & in
as the thrice blessed Hermes
says, and all the sages know
the same above as here below,
the galaxy a holy show.

Elements of the Luberon

1

Several white butterflies
criss-cross over a row
of frilly cabbages;
                    yachts
tacking on an inland sea.

2

The sunflower
displays its flaming heart:
a child's design
in yellow chalk.

3

Mont Ventoux, that still mountain,
lit by the pallor of a thunder clap;
lightning governs the universe!

4

Moss-bearded platforms
          of the great mill
at Isle-sur-Sorgue,
          its cog wheel
creaking slowly,
          air streaming water,
water dripping light:
          the moist centre
of this fecund world.

A Fertile Balance

1

The ring of pure light
on the table, bread and wine,
under the roof of baked tiles,
rooms cool as a pantry.
Stiff dried flowers and herbs
spice the oak beam's
fertile balance: an interior garden.

2

Leaving, returning,
a round of ritual visits:
a tree creaks its slow greeting,
a windlass well, long deserted,
thickets of odorous lavender,
perfumed stone, a spade laid
in drills of aubergine, dense
and dark as hand grenades.

3

A half century ago, the poet
hides in the brush, rifle
butt cradled against shoulder,
as the German convoy grinds near:
before he orders 'Fire!'
a brief scent of wild thyme.

4

A warm day, the ochre earth
leaps before us: the khaki back,
bulging eye, of the cricket,
lofting away like a tiny helicopter
at an angle on its spindle legs.
The shrewd-eyed lizard sprawls,
then darts along a corbelled wall
in a continuous thrum of flies.

5

Now the tall poet greets us
under his lintel, speaking
of rare flowers, scarce birds,
pollution in the rivers great
and small, the muscled Seine,
his homely Sorgue, the sun
on those waters darkening
as the trout turns belly up.

6

'In the land of the day before
the thunder rang pure in the streams,
the vine fostered the bee,
the shoulder lifted the burden.'
Now rocket ranges in the Vaucluse,
the stink of Rhone Poulenc.

'Voters, students of your townland,
of its beasts and flowers, do not
falter in your duty. This is a call
to order, to halt the march of death.'

7

Starless night over the Luberon,
the drone of a friendly plane,
a blossoming of parachutes;
the watchdog lopes between
them, nuzzling their freight
of guns and grenades, but
making no sound, neither bark
nor whimper, before dropping
to sleep on the crumpled silk.

8

'I try not to go to Paris now,
source and centre of all this filth.'
Petrarch, fleeing southwards;
To redeem myself from that
pit of iniquity called Avignon
I fled to where a slate-blue
and white fountain pours,
while birds circle the cliff,
and drank till I felt restored.
Now when I make love
it is for the last time.

Demolition Ireland

for Sybil

Observe the giant machines trundle over
this craggy land, crushing old contours,
trampling down the nearly naked earth.
Dragon rocks dragged into the open,
dislodged from their primaeval dream.
Riverbanks, so slowly, lushly formed,
haunt of the otter and waterhen,
bulldozed into a stern, straight line;
dark trout pools dredged clean
so that doomed cattle may drink any time.
Once mysteries coiled in the tangled clefts
of weed and whin, land left to itself . . .
But see, the rushes rise again, by stealth,
tireless warriors, on the earth's behalf.

The Listeners: Elizabeth's Dream

A deep golden light
on our secret copse:
a flow of honey.

Frost sheathes
each stalk of grass:
a brittle pelt.

Two slender metal
sickle shapes
incline together.

In a gilded mist
of winter sun
they sway and tilt

while the wind whispers,
as in a dance,
as in a trance.

Born from their inter-
secting arcs, a frail
spirit child of steel.

Last of the House

The mountains drowse
around us, each evening.
We almost understand them,

their gorse-tough slopes,
where more has happened
than we can grasp.

In this valley, no one
lifts a fiddle, and no
one speaks Irish.

Though once we heard
Mount Gabriel singing
for an O'Driscoll dying,

the last of his house.
Even the sheep, still
as boulders on the slopes,

lifted their heads
to attend this numinous sound.
Interweaving voices, male

and female, echoing
from the mountain side;
a spectral opera

of loving sorrow;
fierce calamity,
stubborn continuity.

PART THREE

Legerdemain

The wind pushes my body, back.
We are on the way home from Clarkes'
and the winter night streams black

rain, while gusts whip across
the whins, thorns, flailing salleys,
and all those stories we have heard

grouped around that glimmering fireside
as the turf ash fell, and glowed,
now haunt this lightless road.

The knocks in that Cooneen household
that stalked them across the known world.
The farmhand hanging in the yard.

And, the mysterious brass-bound book
from which howling demons awoke
like the headless, headlong horseman

or the rush of the death coach.
Which now shudders behind us
beyond the circle of our tiny torch.

Scraping the Pot

I knelt by my bedside every night
to beg forgiveness for every petty act
against life, beating the dog,
or, more seriously, striking some
senior being across the arm
in the throes of a tantrum,
like my old aunt, bony and sweet
(that memory can still hurt),
and never doubted once
that from some azure heaven
a merciful Christ looked down.

His face loomed nearest
when I crossed the aisles
of our cold chapel in Garvaghey
to kneel in line for Confession.
(It began when I was seven
and had reached the Age of Reason.)
The grille sliding, the probing whisper,
the halting story to that bowed shadow.
Finally, the Act of Contrition,
that strange lightheadedness
of release, after the Blessing.

Scraping the pot, the country
people called it, and
I saw my neighbours' souls
hanging above the hearth,
scoured and gleaming.

Family Rosary

1

The rasp and scrape of wood on stone.
We kneel in a circle of chairs.
Aunt Brigid's has a broken frame,
Aunt Freda steadies a rocker's crescent.
I scuff the arm of a threadbare armchair.

❖

As the steady drone deepens,
Hail Mary dissolving into Holy Mary,
I bury my head in the musty cushions,
tease their tassels in boyish boredom

until Aunt Brigid leads the final prayers,
a voice raised against the night,
assuming response, numbering the dead
with claim on these frail living,

who sigh in their separate reveries
of Sorrowful and Joyful mysteries
while the beads glide through fingers —
grain sliding from a sack.

❖

And the walls fade and change,
the lights dwindle under the holy picture
with its soft pierced hands;
the fire is sucked up the chimney,
the traffic swallows the road.

2 the trimmings

Garrulous Berryman, break the Mississippi ice
like a seal, with a fresh sonnet for us;
strict Marianne, sport your black cartwheel
of a hat again, at Ebbet's Field:

Señor Graves, lead the company gladly,
in Cork or Mallorca, with an Irish *come-all-ye*,
MacDiarmid, with tough terrier intensity,
share a rare Highland Malt with us,

while Austin, lover of Erato, lifts
a thin glass, a Winter's Tale, and
David Jones and his crony, René,
grow merry upon Rose's Lime Juice Cordial.

Now that my admired dead begin
to overtake the living, I might muster
a new litany of ghostly recruits
so that all the good and gifted dead
may strengthen the hands of the living:
to work as well, in death's shade,
and not lose heart, or faith.

Wreaths

1 a good bye

René Hague, you endured your hospital bed
with thin rolled cigarettes, and mild soldier's curses,
until they informed you that your wife was dead
and your own disease, terminal. Then you turned
your lean face to the wall, after a formal farewell:

you gave me back the books you had borrowed,
George Herbert's *The Temple*, and Dante's *Paradiso*,
then, lifting my hand to your sere lips,
sighed *Goodbye*. The memory of such grace
is like a rare liqueur from which memory sips.

2 civil war veteran

i.m. C S (Todd) Andrews

At the cigar and brandy stage,
an old civil war veteran recalls
someone he killed — a half secret —
or someone he missed — a half regret.

Somehow, it now amounts to the same thing.
'Sure, he'd be dead, or —' (half-laughing,
blinking age-cowled saurian eyes)
' — half dying now, like myself.'

Grave Song

So many deaths
wear the heart away
or grind it to a halt
a while, to start again
in a different way:
having lost for a time
its sense of itself,
the unique burden
of a particular life.

But the form
is solid enough, sound
as an old church bell
and a tune wells up
deeper, stronger
that does not deny
the sombre sunken message
of that burial ground:

where the grave lay open,
yes, but to the open sky.

Last Court

Poetry, 'tis a court of judgement upon the soul.
                                    — Henrik Ibsen

1
Non piangere

From your last chair,
two months before that glutton, cancer,
devoured you, lawyer brother,
you gave me a final wigging, read the riot act,
as if I were some juvenile delinquent
hauled before the magistrate.

This sun-warm conservatory,
latest addition to your ultra-modern bungalow
overlooking Brown-Lecky's estate,
(now manicured golf course) recalls the deck
of that Cunard liner, the *Cameronia*,
which, ages ago, shipped us boys to Fintona.

Home again, in mid-Tyrone,
you built your now fading life,
fathering a tribe within a tribe,
only to chide me now, for my 'great mistake,
repeated, *twice*', of choosing a wife
from the wider world outside.

'They don't understand. You need somebody
who thinks like you, shares your beliefs.'
Mildly, I place a picture of your two nieces
(my Cork, French, Jewish,
Church of Ireland children)
upon your knee, for loving avuncular scrutiny.

But you sigh it away
and, having pronounced your last verdict,
stalk off to rest, dying, but striding with dignity,
without a whimper of self-pity,
through your assembled family,
your last gift, this fragile bravery.

2

To leave me forever, with your disapproval,
yet rueful love, and a contradictory testimony,
'Strangely, I have never felt so happy, as now,
giving up, letting go, floating free.'
You look down, pensively, at your glass
of burnished Black Bush whiskey.

'And, no, I no longer pray,
although I talk to God sometimes in my head.
And our parents. Why did you hurt our mother's pride
with your mournful auld poem, *The Dead Kingdom*?
Only a child, you couldn't understand their decision:
besides, you got the details wrong!'

'So you believe we'll see them again?
Bone-light, transfigured, Molly and Jim,
angels dancing upon a pin, and then
I can take it up with them again?'
'No,' you say stubbornly, 'never again,'
shaking your once-red Ulster head.

And plucking your pallid, freckled arm,
'I don't believe,' you proclaim,
'in the body's resurrection.
See how the flesh wastes parchment-thin?'
Yet, resigned as the Dying Gaul,
stoic as an ancient Roman.

3

Un grido lacerante

Dear freckled brother, in an old photo,
you throw your arm around me
in a Brooklyn park, your impulse to hug
preserved there for posterity.
Let me reverse our roles, carefully as I can,
to encircle you, this time, with *my* arm.

In far off Florence, I learnt of your death;
Evelyn calling from a rain-swept West Cork.
'It was a merciful release,' that cliché — yet true.
'But how can I trek all that way North?
My sister's children are here, as well as our own.
It's a long hard slog up to County Tyrone.'

Phone to my ear, gazing out at the Arno,
I hear, behind her, the laughter of children,
those nieces whose picture you dismissed.
'Cherish the living, while honouring the dead,
I'll stand over that, pray they'll comprehend.
The church bells of Florence will bless him instead.'

As many mourners assemble at your funeral
in our chill and distant Northern chapel
since you loved paintings I patrol
the Pitti, the Uffizi, turning from
a foam-borne Botticelli nymph, or
grave Madonna, to weep above Dante's city:

sharp-tempered, once you smashed me to the floor
in our mother's kitchen, and standing over
me, like some American boxer, 'Rise
and fight like a man' — and I only sixteen!
Aproned Molly hovering, a hapless referee;
you stalk away, to return with a brusque apology.

Sharp-tempered but kindly, you drove
your poet brother home from Dublin,
emptying my squalid flat without reproach.
Later, wives and lives came between us,
differing codes of conduct and belief.
Yet I still glimpse your ginger hair and freckle face.

Long before the cancer struck, I saw that face
grown ashen, fissured as chalk, suddenly old
as though some secret source had parched,
and sought to tell you, *Relax again,*
as when you roamed Bundoran with the Fintona gang.
But tact forbade. Or cowardice?

Now, hear my plea. Sweet-souled Santayana
might have agreed with you, brother, about exogamy,
but against your patriarchal views,
I assert the right of love to choose,
from whatever race, or place. And of verse
to allay, to heal, our tribal curse, that narrowness.

First Landscape, First Death

So deep this landscape lies
in me; I try to leave it behind,
but again and again it returns,
burning with its secret light.

       Russet bog
loses itself in a blue distance,
a curlew laments overhead,
and again I become that displaced
child, wandering these lanes, break-
ing a stick from these hedges,
to lash the crowns off thistles,
pressing purple foxglove fingers
together, to yield a brief burst
of sound, exploring the mystery
of an old limekiln, where a heifer
licks her calf.

       My father
wanted to be buried here
and before Aunt Mary died
she asked her son to drive her
around these same rough hills
(but with their secret lushness),
after the hard care of marriage
and children, to re-find the girl
who once wandered there.

❖

Big Allie Owens crunched down
the lane in her high-buttoned boots
to collect her pension and provisions.

When she grew too old, I had
to haul the basket to her. Thick
crusted shop bread, planks of ribboned
bacon, fed that mare's stomach:
oven and skillet suspended
on black hooks over a turf fire.

Abandoned by her doctor,
the priest came to reconcile her,
to measure her, for the long fight
towards death. I sat by her bedside
after school, watching the dark grow
against the pines, where the crows
sank to rest, and heard her groan
against her fate. Large-limbed
as a cart horse, she died hard.

But first, slowly, she gave away
all she had to her neighbours.
I got a shoal of bright half-crowns,
but to Kitty Horisk, with her children,
'There's a wheen of sovereigns
under the mattress, all for you.'
For everyone, something. And still
they came, competing in friendliness,
carrying sweet water from the well,
new wheaten bread, until the end.

❖

So, for myself, I would seek
no other final home, than
this remote country hiding place,
which gave me gentle nourishment
when I was most in need of it;

and still gives solace. In dream
I leap across stone through stream,
stride from road to lane. And even
moving light-footed between
cities where I am known
I am stopped suddenly by
the sight of some distant hill
or curving twilight river, to see
on a ghostly mound, my abiding
symbol, a weathered standing stone.

Slievemore

1

When this landscape has been
   absorbed into the mind
   taken up into the dream

a single image may flake
   away, flint or obsidian,
   to reveal a whole civilization.

2

Called up
by thunder clap
by draughts of rain

the bronze doors
of the evening sky open
and I shiver to discern

massively
glinting in the watery sun:
Slievemore's guardian forms.

3

Jagged head
of warrior, bird
of prey, surveying space

side by side
they squat, the stern
deities of this place,

giant arms
slant to the calm
of lap, kneebone;

blunt fingers
splay to caress
a rain-hollowed stone

towards which
the landscape of five parishes
tends, band after band

of final,
peewit haunted,
cropless bogland.

PART FOUR

The Plain of Blood

But darkness was here yesterday.
— Joseph Conrad

*Irish culture is a great deal older than Christianity and
people were buried so that they could face the rising sun.*
— John McGahern

Crom Cruach or *Dubh*,
the crooked or dark one:
our most fearsome legend.

We went in search of him
one summer, from Sligo,
near Loughs Allen and Arrow,
halting to follow the lost
stone alignments of Moytura,
boulders strewn, like playthings
of some giant's giant whim,
now obscured by stubborn whin.
This mythic battleground,
a smothered Carnac, yet beyond,
homely hayricks, moored by
stones, cluster in the tiny fields.

(Into one of which we now
climb, across a wooden stile
to fulfil an old erotic dream,
shortening a mile, by lying
against the bristling warmth
of a small, domed haycock.
The redolence of the day,
earth, grass, sun-bleached hay,
stirs us to a quick kindling
before we take, again, our way.)

An aroma of wildflowers
and the mind's root stirs,
door after door opening
inside the head, till we are
on some pilgrimage of legend,
this small corner of our small
country, as warm and lovely now
as it can be melancholy: a dark
or sunlit island. Do we journey
in a car, or a brazen chariot?

❖

My face lifted to the sun.
I ride in my open car:
the wings of the imagination open;
I am a warrior at the helm,
Cuchulainn or great Fionn?

Then, an unexpected find,
or gift, beyond Arigna's coalfield,
a roadside memorial to Carolan.
The blind harper's last refrain,
turning his horse towards Ballyfarnon,
'After all I've gone through,
to die at home at last.' And
die he did on Lady Day,
at the house of his patrons;
chanting a final quatrain, before
the last pluck of the harpstring.

His four-day wake another legend,
mourners swelling the small town,
with tents for the poorer folks,
a keg of rough whiskey

each side of the hall door,
a flotilla of harpers, and
his noble patroness crying
'over her poor gentleman'.
Crying, playing and celebrating
(one patroness sobbing,
two caggs a' flowing,
four days a' drinking,
ten players a' playing),
and a blind harper
still singing underground.

❖

We pick up an elderly hitch-hiker
intent on the local pub.
Scenting a new audience
he tells an old story about
Kilronan, the church of Ronan
who, surprisingly, had a daughter
honoured by the wayside
well and shrine of St Lasair.
'There's great healing there,
if you bless the forehead,
and pass between the stones.'
Then, eyeing my companion,
her looks fair and Anglo-Saxon,
he risks a moral tale of how
a drunken landlord riding home
dismounted to defile the well.
'He loosed his trousers where
St Ronan's daughter, that holy girl,
had prayed to heal us all.' With
the skill of a seasoned storyteller
he pauses to read our expression,

then with a wicked flourish,
'From that day to this, never,
again, could he shit or piss!'

Drover's stick, hat and all, stumbling
from the car, he gives his blessing
by the roadside, in Manorhamilton,
'I've a feeling you'll find today
whatever you may be looking for.'
And so we seem to do, nearing
our journey's end in Ballymacgovern,
seeking the townland of Moyslacht
(the Plain of Blood, or Slaughter),
hardly an ordinary request, or quest?

The strong farmer in the dark pub,
stick nestled between his knees,
slowly lifts a pint as black
as his own serge suit,
as comfortable as the watch fob
anchored on his waistcoat,
and tells us he knows nothing,
but gestures towards a gnome
seated near the big counter:
'I think you've found your man.
He knows everything here, around.'

And miraculously he did,
leading us down the road
to where a stone keep holds
a hill. 'Are you sure it's not
the castle of the MacGoverns
you came looking for?' But,
after that sly askance,
he brings us along a hidden lane,

heavy with blackberries, to where
a small mound rises, crowned by
a circlet of crooked trees.
'He's up there, if he's anywhere,
and if you forage round the base
you'll find the lesser ones.'

As indeed we do, tracing a fort
inside the hilltop grove, and tracks
of twelve stones, in the weeds about.
A central figure, with twelve apostles;
a humbler version of the Christian myth?
On the fort's edge, our guide stands poised.
'There's them,' he says, 'that believe
there was no human sacrifice, there was
no Plain of Slaughter or Blood.
'Twas all invented by the Christians
to change old gods into new demons.
You see that bush we passed below?
When St Patrick came to see the Crom
the druids sent a squall of rain.
But when the saint took shelter
the fuschia sprang open, like an umbrella,
to protect the holy fella!

                              'It depends,
I suppose, what side you're on.
Look from this hilltop, and you'll see
fort after fort, crowning the hills, all the way
across, as far as Clogher in Tyrone,
where they had the Golden Stone:
do you happen to know where I mean?'
(That sidelong glance again.)
'Sure, it's only a step to the border.
They were all one people living here,

and on these hills they said their prayer.
They hoisted this stone upright there
long before the Christians came.
Legend says those that built them
were small and dark, like me, not tall
and blue-eyed, like you.'

And he smiles.
Together we gaze across the landscape,
mound folding into mound, hillocks
moulded in a time of ice, now green
and golden with harvest.

Still hard to credit;
since death is general,
blemishing our North,
that blood-boltered earth.
Libations poured daily:
Our Father, who dwells
in darkness, grant us this day
our daily dread!

Yet
a pet of a day; our dark island
as warm and lovely now
as it can be melancholy;
terror and beauty suspended
in this heavy summer air,
and an illumination pierces:

here was no sullen dark god,
but a shining central stone
with its monthly attendants:
the Sun God and His seasons,
an Irish Apollo pouring

down His daily benison.
Where three counties
sweep to meet, I dream
a lucent standing stone
with all its children, men
and women, summoning
the blessing of the sun.

❖

The wings of the imagination
are slowly folding in:
our guide escorts us down
to our sunlit chariot
(in fact, a rackety Austin).
'And what brought you here?'
he asks, accepting the coin.
'We never see anyone.'

I open all my *Guides*
one by one, but his eyes slide,
like pebbles, down the page.
That gaze, so shrewd and lively
on the knoll, is blinkered now:
our Virgil cannot read!

Wandering back, our journey done,
we wheel the car windows down
and smell new-cut grass, fern,
that coconut spice of whin,
and an unexpected scent, like roses,
everywhere. At the last turn,

the humped shape of Ben Bulben,
brooding over Sligo town.
But that is a myth from an older pen,
and all this never happened,
or was told by a doting man?

Acknowledgements and Notes

Most of these poems were first seen by my partner, Elizabeth Wassell, whose wordhoard helped to shape them. Acknowledgements are also due to the editors and publishers of *Agenda*, *Exile* (Toronto), *Firebird*, *The Honest Ulsterman*, *Irish Pages*, *The Irish University Review*, *The Irish Times*, *Metre*, *Poetry* (Chicago), *The Shop*, and *The Times Literary Supplement*.

'The Plain of Blood' was translated into French by Philippe Démeron and published in *Les Citadelles*.

The title *Drunken Sailor* is not only a sea shanty but also a hornpipe from *O'Neill's Dance Music of Ireland* (1907).

page 29   A ninth-century Irish poem, known as 'The Scribe in the Woods', opens with the line *'Dom-fharcai fidbaide fál'* (A hedge of trees above me).

page 35   Based on *Dinnscheanchas* or Place Wisdom, place names gathered by the folklorist, Gearóid Ó Crualaoich.

page 36   The Angelus sounds throughout the Republic, not only from church steeples, but also on the national radio and television, at noon and 6 pm, accompanied on television by images. This practice has provoked some predictable criticism in the Paisleyite North, but also from those in the Republic devoted to the separation of Church and State in a new and more ethnically diverse Ireland.

page 47   The title 'Last of the House' is based on the Irish phrase *An Fear Deireanach den tSloinneadh* (The Last of that Family Name).

page 54   'The Trimmings' were prayers for the dead added after the Family Rosary in the Catholic Ireland of my youth.

page 60   George Santayana (1863-1952) was of Spanish background and taught philosophy at his alma mater, Harvard University: Wallace Stevens was influenced by his thinking. Although Santayana himself never married, he cherished surprisingly strict and conventional views on marriage.